l.c. 3/16

Emancipation

Proclamation

and the

13th, 14th & 15th

Amendments

Written by Douglas M. Rife

Illustrated by Bron Smith

D0874932

Teaching & Learning Company

1204 Buchanan St., P.O. Box 10
Carthage, IL 62321-0010

This book belongs to

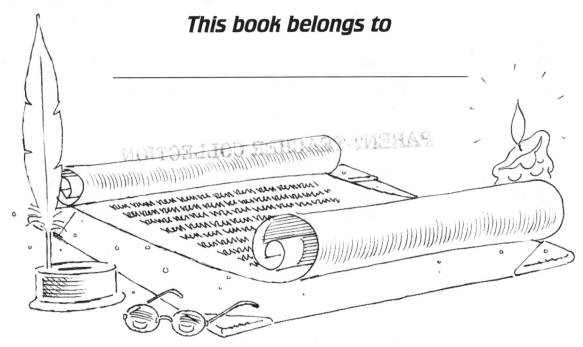

For Zain Rife.

I would like to thank Cindy VanHorn at the Lincoln Museum in Fort Wayne, Indiana, for her assistance with the prints in this book.

Cover photo courtesy of Images of American Political History. All images are believed to be in the public domain.

Every attempt has been made to contact and secure permission for any copyrighted material in this book. Please contact the publisher if any item has inadvertently been overlooked.

ISBN No. 1-57310-349-7

Printing No. 987654321

Teaching & Learning Company
1204 Buchanan St., P.O. Box 10
Carthage, IL 62321-0010

Table of Contents

Objectives 5

Introduction to the Emancipation
Proclamation   *Handout 1* 6

The Emancipation Proclamation Time Line
Handout 2 9

Civil War Map Activity   *Handout 3* 10

Emancipation Proclamation   *Handout 4* . . . 11

Understanding the Emancipation
Proclamation   *Handout 5* 12

Proclamation Crossword   *Handout 6* 13

Thirteenth, Fourteenth and
Fifteenth Amendments   *To the Teacher* . 14

Thirteenth, Fourteenth
and Fifteenth Amendments   *Handout 7* 15

Amendment Match   *Handout 8* 16

Amendment Review   *Handout 9* 17

The Poetry of Lincoln   *To the Teacher* 19

From A Poem by James Monroe Whitfield
Handout 10 20

Understanding A Poem by James
Monroe Whitfield *Handout 11* 21

"The Emancipation Group" by John
Greenleaf Whittier *Handout 12* 22

Understanding "The Emancipation
Group" by John Greenleaf
Whittier *Handout 13* 23

Editorial Cartoons   *To the Teacher* 24

Understanding Abraham Lincoln's Last Card
or Rouge-et-Noir   *Handout 14* 26

"Freedom to the Slaves" by Currier & Ives
Handout 15 27

Understanding "Freedom to the Slaves"
by Currier & Ives   *Handout 16* 28

"Writing the Emancipation Proclamation"
by Adalbert Joann Volck   *Handout 17* . . 29

Understanding "Writing the Emancipation
Proclamation" by Adalbert Joann Volck
Handout 18 30

Answer Key 31

Dear Teacher or Parent,

The Emancipation Proclamation represents a turning point in the Civil War. Though many historians argue that the decree did not actually grant freedom to a single slave, it did give hope to millions bound in that "peculiar institution."

Abraham Lincoln, as commander in chief of the armed forces prosecuting the war, had to walk a delicate balance between the abolitionists who wanted a declaration freeing all of the slaves and keeping those living in the slave-holding border states of Missouri, Kentucky, Delaware and Maryland in the Union. Lincoln, therefore, struck a balance that neither pleased the abolitionists nor freed the slaves in any but the Southern States in areas that were not controlled by Union forces. This compromise move, however, had the moral force it needed to keep Great Britain from an alliance with the South. It also sounded the death knell to slavery. Most people realized at the time that the Proclamation was the beginning of the end of slavery.

The purpose of this book is to provide a brief history of the Proclamation, as well as a better understanding of the document itself through activities that help students focus on its meaning and impact. The book introduces the Thirteenth, Fourteenth and Fifteenth Amendments to students as further illustrations of the long-term effects of Lincoln's impact on the United States Constitution and our history. The spirit of the Proclamation is imbedded in those amendments.

Also included are two poems that celebrate Lincoln and the Emancipation Proclamation. The first, *A Poem* by James Monroe Whitfield, was written to commemorate a statue of Lincoln. The second poem was written by a former slave, John Greenleaf Whittier, to celebrate the 14th anniversary of the Proclamation. The book also includes a British editorial cartoon that first appeared in the English magazine *Punch* shortly after the Preliminary Emancipation Proclamation was issued. The cartoon illustrates the view of some English that the Proclamation was an act of political desperation that was a gamble that was not going to succeed. The last two activities literally "illustrate" opposing views of Lincoln and the Emancipation Proclamation.

Sincerely,

Douglas M. Rife

Objectives

After completing the following activities	the students should be able to . . .
The Emancipation Proclamation	1. place the Emancipation Proclamation in a larger historical context 2. explain the impact of the document 3. identify the northern, southern and border states
The Thirteenth, Fourteenth and Fifteenth Amendments	1. introduce students to the Thirteenth, Fourteenth and Fifteenth Amendments of the Constitution 2. understand the meaning of the amendments
Civil War Era Poetry	1. identify imagery 2. interpret symbolism 3. explain the poet's references
Images of Lincoln and the Emancipation Proclamation	1. identify caricature 2. identify symbolism 3. draw conclusions about the meaning in a cartoon or print 4. identify differing opinions 5. draw own editorial cartoons 6. judge the cartoonist's viewpoint

Introduction to the Emancipation Proclamation

The debate in the United States about slavery had been taking place since the very beginning of the formation of the country. In fact, the first debates about slavery took place as the Constitution was being written. The debate continued as states were admitted to the Union. Slave and free states were admitted in equal numbers to ensure that neither faction, slave nor free had a majority in the United States Senate. The first crisis took place in 1820 concerning the admittance of Missouri. To maintain the balance in the Senate, Missouri was admitted as a slave state and Maine was admitted as a free state. Much of the debate centered around a state's right to decide what laws were to be passed inside a state's borders. The next big crisis erupted in 1850 with the admittance of California as a free state. As a compromise, territorial governments were set up in the territories ceded by the Mexican government after the Mexican-American War and were given the authority to decide the slavery question for themselves.

By the time of the 1860 election, the free and the slave states had clear positions in the ensuing debate. The free states consisted of Maine, Vermont, New Hampshire, Rhode Island, New York, Massachusetts, Connecticut, New Jersey, Pennsylvania, Ohio, Michigan, Wisconsin, Indiana, Illinois, Iowa, Oregon, Kansas and California. The slave states consisted of Maryland, Delaware, Virginia, Kentucky, Missouri, Tennessee, North Carolina, South Carolina, Arkansas, Texas, Louisiana, Mississippi, Alabama, Georgia and Florida.

The election of 1860 was a hotly debated and contested election. The Republicans nominated Abraham Lincoln as their presidential candidate. Lincoln had become famous during his bid for the Illinois senate race against Stephen A. Douglas, a leading Democrat. Lincoln spoke out against the immorality of slavery, while Douglas defended his philosophy of popular sovereignty, that is that the people of a state should decide the issue of slavery for themselves. The Democrats split, however. The Southern Democrats would not support Senator Stephen A. Douglas from Illinois, who won the nomination. The Southern Democrats left the convention and nominated John C. Breckinridge in a separate convention. Another party, the Constitutional Union Party, nominated John Bell of Tennessee.

1860

November Abraham Lincoln was elected President of the United States. Lincoln received 1,866,452 votes; Douglas received 1,376,957 votes; Breckinridge received 849,781 votes and Bell received 588,879 votes.

December 20 South Carolina seceded from the Union, becoming the first state to do so. In their convention, the vote was unanimous, 169 to 0. Succession Conventions took place all through the South.

Introduction to the Emancipation Proclamation

1861

January 9   Mississippi seceded from the Union in an 84 to 15 vote.

January 10   Florida seceded, 62 to 7.

January 11   Alabama seceded, 61 to 39.

January 19   Georgia seceded, 209 to 89.

January 26   Louisiana seceded, 113 to 17.

February 1   Texas seceded, 166 to 7.

February 8   The Confederate States of America adopted a Constitution.

February 9   Jefferson Davis became president of the Confederate States of America.

February 18   Jefferson Davis was inaugurated President of the Confederate States of America.

March 6   Abraham Lincoln was inaugurated President of the United States in Washington, D.C.

April 12   Confederate soldiers under the command of General Pierre Beauregard attacked Fort Sumter in Charleston, South Carolina, with a barrage of cannon fire marking the beginning of the Civil War.

April 17   In a second succession convention, Virginia seceded by a vote of 88 to 55, delegates from the western part of the state walked out saying they would form a pro-Union state government.

April 19   President Lincoln declared a naval blockade against southern ports to block imports that would aid the South in its efforts to persecute the war.

May 6   Tennessee, 66 to 25, and Arkansas, 69 to 1, seceded.

May 20   North Carolina seceded in an unanimous vote from the Union, becoming the last state to join the Confederacy. Four slave states—Delaware, Maryland, Missouri and Kentucky—did not join the Confederate states.

July 21   The Union Army lost the first battle of the war at Bull Run, only 25 miles from Washington, D.C.

Introduction to the Emancipation Proclamation

October 24 Representatives from nearly 40 counties in western Virginia approved the formation of a pro-Union state.

1862

March 31 Lincoln signed into law a bill that prohibited Union army or navy personnel from returning any runaway slaves to their owners. In June the United States entered into a treaty with Great Britain allowing each country to search the others' vessels in the waters off the coast of Africa for Africans bound for the slave market. This was a big blow to the slave traders because it interrupted the flow of slaves into the southern states.

April 6-7 General Grant and his troops were surprised by Confederate forces at Shiloh. Thirteen thousand Union troops were killed and wounded with 10,000 Confederate troops dead and wounded.

April 16 Lincoln signed a bill outlawing slavery in the District of Columbia. The bill also provided $300 compensation per slave to any slaveholder affected by the act. According to Massachusetts Senator Charles Sumner, Lincoln had been the largest slaveholder in the country, "for he holds 300,000 slaves of the District of Columbia."

July 22 Lincoln called a cabinet meeting where he proposed issuing a proclamation to emancipate the slaves in all states where they were in open insurrection against the United States government. The cabinet discussed the proclamation. William Seward, who was Secretary of State, believed the proclamation was the correct thing to do but argued that it should be issued after a major victory by Union forces. In that way, President Lincoln would be making the proclamation from a position of power and strength.

September 17 Union forces stopped General Lee and his troops at one of the bloodiest battles of the war at Antietam Creek, Maryland. Over 26,000 men were killed, wounded or missing. General Lee and his men retreated across the Potomac River into Virginia to escape.

September 22 President Abraham Lincoln issued the Preliminary Emancipation Proclamation.

December 13 The Union forces lost at the battle of Fredericksburg, Virginia.

1863

January 1 President Lincoln issued the final Emancipation Proclamation.

Name _____

The Emancipation Proclamation Time Line

Place the following events on the time line next to the years in which they occurred.

- South Carolina secedes from the Union
- Emancipation Proclamation issued
- Fort Sumter attacked
- Abraham Lincoln elected President of the United States
- Preliminary Emancipation Proclamation issued
- Confederate States adopt a Constitution

November 1860— _____

December 1860— _____

February 1861— _____

April 1861— _____

September 1862— _____

January 1863— _____

Civil War Map Activity

Read the "Introduction to the Emancipation Proclamation" handouts and label the map.

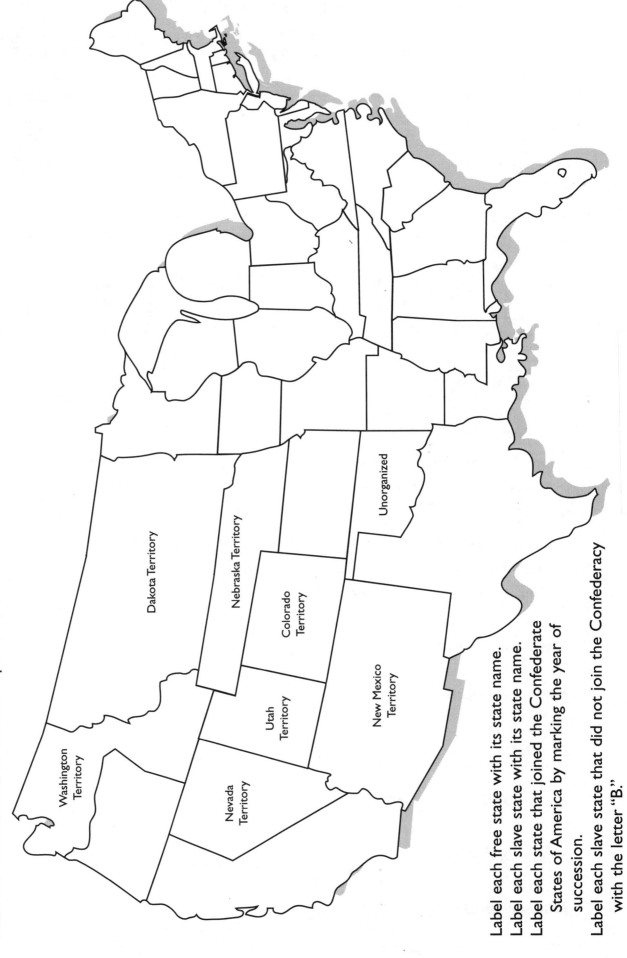

Label each free state with its state name.
Label each slave state with its state name.
Label each state that joined the Confederate
States of America by marking the year of
succession.
Label each slave state that did not join the Confederacy
with the letter "B."

Handout 3

Emancipation Proclamation

1) Whereas on the 22nd day of September, A.D. 1862, a proclamation was issued by the President of the United States, containing among other things, the following, to wit:

2) "That on the 1st day of January, A.D. 1863, all persons held as slaves within any State or designated part of a State the people whereof shall then be in rebellion against the United States shall be then, thenceforward, and forever free; and the executive government of the United States including the military and naval authority thereof, will recognize and maintain the freedom of such persons and will do no acts or acts to repress such persons, or any of them, in any efforts they may make for their actual freedom.

3) "That the executive will on the 1st day of January aforesaid, by proclamation, designate the States and parts of States, if any, in which the people thereof, respectively, shall then be in rebellion against the United States; and the fact that any State or the people thereof shall on that day be in good faith represented in the Congress of the United States by members chosen thereto at elections wherein a majority of the qualified voters of such States shall have participated shall, in the absence of strong countervailing testimony, be deemed conclusive evidence that such State and the people thereof are not then in rebellion against the United States."

4) Now, therefore, I, Abraham Lincoln, President of the Untied States, by virtue of the power in me vested as Commander-in-Chief of the Army and Navy of the United States in time of actual armed rebellion against the authority and government of the United States, and as a fit measure for suppressing said rebellion, do, on this 1st day of January, A. D. 1863, and in accordance with my purpose so to do, publicly proclaimed for the full period of one hundred days from the first day above mentioned, order and designate as the States and parts of the States wherein the people thereof, respectively, are this day in rebellion against the United States the following, to wit:

5) Arkansas, Texas, Louisiana (except the parishes of St. Bernard, Plaquemines, Jefferson, St. John, St. Charles, St. James, Ascension, Assumption, Terrebonne, Lafourche, St. Mary, St. Martin, and Orleans, including the city of New Orleans), Mississippi, Alabama, Florida, Georgia, South Carolina, North Carolina, and Virginia (except the forty-eight counties designated as West Virginia, and also the counties of Berkeley, Accomac, Northhampton, Elizabeth City, York, Princess Anne, and Northfolk, including the cities of Northfolk and Portsmouth), and which excepted parts are for the present left precisely as if this proclamation were not issued.

6) And by virtue of the power and for the purpose aforesaid, I do order and declare that all persons held as slaves within said designated States and parts of States are, and henceforward shall be free; and that the Executive Government of the United States, including the military and naval authorities thereof, will recognize and maintain the freedom of said persons.

7) And I hereby enjoin upon the people so declared to be free to abstain from all violence, unless in necessary self-defense; and I recommend to them that, in all cases when allowed, they labor faithfully for reasonable wages.

8) And I further declare and make known that such persons of suitable condition will be received into the armed service of the United States to garrison forts, positions, stations, and other places, and to man vessels of all sorts in said service.

9) And upon this act, sincerely believed to be an act of justice, warranted by the Constitution upon military necessity, I invoke the considerate judgment of mankind and the gracious favor of Almighty God.

10) In witness whereof, I have hereunto set my hand and caused the seal of the United States to be affixed.

11) Done at the City of Washington, this first day of January, in the year of our Lord one thousand eight hundred and sixty-three, and of the Independence of the United States of America the eighty-seventh.

By the President Abraham Lincoln
-William H. Seward, Secretary of State

Name _____

Understanding the Emancipation Proclamation

1. Look up the word *emancipation*. Define it in your own words. _____
   _____

2. Look up *proclamation*. Define it in your own words. _____
   _____

3. When was the preliminary proclamation issued? _____

4. When did the full proclamation take effect? _____

5. Paragraph 2 has two clauses. Explain the substance of each clause in your own words.
   _____

6. To what does the word *rebellion* refer? _____

7. In the first clause of paragraph 3, the Proclamation states that the executive will designate which states are in rebellion. How does clause 2 define this? _____

8. Who issued the proclamation? _____

9. What government position does the person hold who issued the Proclamation? _____

10. According to the document, what was the reason the Proclamation was issued?
    _____

11. Look at the map of the United States. Which states were chosen in which to declare slaves free? _____

12. Which states were not chosen? _____

13. Why would so-called border states not be included in the Proclamation to grant slaves freedom? Explain your answer. _____
    _____

14. William Seward, Secretary of State said, "We show our sympathy with slavery by emancipating the slaves where we cannot reach them and holding them in bondage where we can set them free." Explain what he meant in regard to the Emancipation Proclamation.
    _____
    _____

15. What two things does the document request of those who have been set free?
    _____

16. What does the Proclamation guarantee to those slaves if they are of "suitable condition"?
    _____

Handout 5

Name _____

Proclamation Crossword

All correct answers will reveal the name of the person who signed the Emancipation Proclamation.

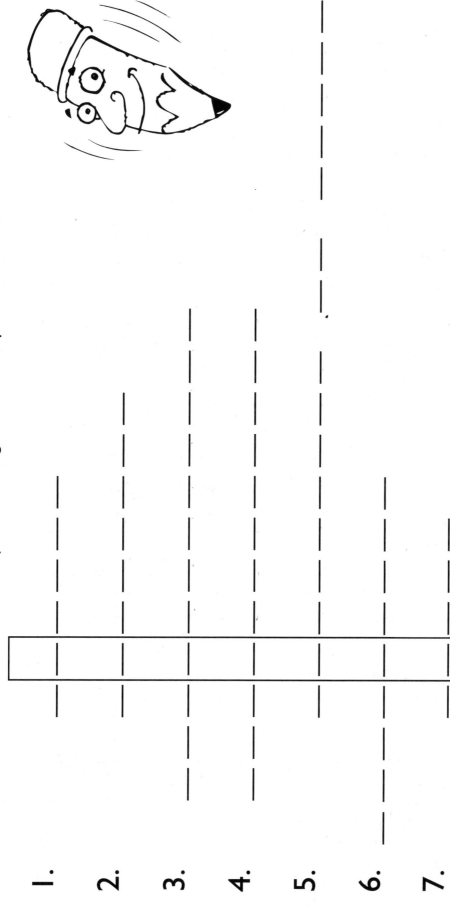

1. _ _ _ _ _ _ _ _ _ _ _ _

2. _ _ _ _ _ _ _ _

3. _ _ _ _ _ _ _ _ _

4. _ _ _ _ _ _ _ _ _ _

5. _ _ _ _ _ _

6. _ _ _ _ _ _ _ _ _ _ _

7. _ _ _ _ _ _ _ _ _ _ _

1. The Emancipation Proclamation freed these in the states in rebellion against the United States.
2. Forty-eight counties of this state made up a new state in 1863.
3. This word means "set free."
4. This word means "public announcement."
5. Abraham Lincoln was not only President but also in charge of the army and navy as _____.
6. Those who were fighting against the Union were said to be in _____.
7. These forces fought Confederate forces.

Thirteenth, Fourteenth & Fifteenth Amendments

Objectives

To introduce students to the 13th, 14th and 15th Amendments of the Constitution.

Understand the meaning of the amendments.

Vocabulary

slavery: the keeping of people in bondage to toil against their will.

involuntary servitude: to work against one's will.

naturalized: to obtain the rights of citizenship.

Background

For more than 60 years no amendments to the Constitution had been proposed. Not since the 12th Amendment had been passed to solve the constitutional crisis caused by the election of 1800, when Thomas Jefferson and Aaron Burr received the same number of electoral votes in the Electoral College.

Toward the end of the Civil War and after, the Radical Republicans dominating Congress began to codify in the Constitution what they had won on the battlefield, namely, the so-called "national supremacy" amendments. The 13th Amendment was proposed to fulfill the intent of the Emancipation Proclamation and guarantee that slavery would be outlawed in the United States by constitutional amendment. The 14th Amendment was written more broadly, and written to guarantee civil rights to the recently emancipated slaves. The 14th Amendment also granted full citizenship rights to African American men and naturalized citizens. The amendment also forbids individual states from making any laws that would abridge the privileges or immunities of citizens of the United States. In other words, states could not deprive their citizens of life, liberty or property without due process of law. This now became a federal guarantee. The amendment also stated that representation in the House of Representatives was going to be based on counting all people equally (except untaxed Indians). This put an end to the enslaved African Americans being counted as three-fifths for purposes of the census. The measure also barred those who had served in the civil government of the Confederacy from serving in the federal government after the war. Congress could waive this restriction from federal office holding with a super-majority of two-thirds. The 15th Amendment was written to guarantee voting rights for African American men 21 years of age.

Suggested Lesson Plan

1. Explain the lesson objectives.
2. Define the lesson vocabulary words.
3. Distribute the handout with the 13th, 14th and 15th Amendments (page 15).
4. Use the sheet to begin discussion about what each amendment means. Ask the students what they think the guarantees are in each amendment.
5. Then distribute the "Amendment Match" handout (page 16) and invite the students to match the amendment to each statement.
6. Distribute the "Amendment Review" handouts (pages 17-18). The review questions can be used to review the questions as a class or individually.

TLC10349 Copyright © Teaching & Learning Company, Carthage, IL 62321-0010

Name _____

Thirteenth, Fourteenth & Fifteenth Amendments

13th Amendment

[Proposed by Congress on January 31, 1865; ratification completed on December 6, 1865.]

Section 1. Neither slavery nor involuntary servitude, except as a punishment for crime whereof the party shall have been duly convicted, shall exist within the United States, or any place subject to their jurisdiction.

Section 2. Congress shall have power to enforce this article by appropriate legislation.

14th Amendment

[Proposed by Congress on June 13, 1866, ratification completed on July 9, 1868.]

Section 1. All persons born or naturalized in the United States, and subject to the jurisdiction thereof, are citizens of the United States and of the State wherein they reside. No State shall make or enforce any law which shall abridge the privileges or immunities of citizens of the United States; nor shall any State deprive any person of life, liberty, or property, without due process of law; nor deny to any person within its jurisdiction the equal protection of the laws.

Section 2. Representatives shall be apportioned among the several States according to their respective numbers, counting the whole number of persons in each State, excluding Indians not taxed. But when the right to vote at any election for the choice of electors for President and Vice president of the United States, Representatives in Congress, the Executive and Judicial officers of a State, or the members of the Legislature thereof, is denied to any of the male inhabitants of such State, being twenty-one years of age, and citizens of the United States, or in any way abridged, except for participation in rebellion, or other crime, the basis of representation therein shall be reduced in the proportion which the number of such male citizens shall bear to the whole number of male citizens twenty-one years of age in such State.

Section 3. No person shall be a Senator or Representative in Congress, or elector of President or Vice President, or hold any office, civil or military, under the United States, or under any State, who, having previously taken an oath, as a member of Congress, or as an officer of the United States, or as a member of any State legislature, or as an executive of judicial officer of any State, to support the Constitution of the United States, shall have engaged in insurrection or rebellion against the same, or given aid or comfort to the enemies thereof. But Congress may by a vote of two-thirds of each House, remove such disability.

Section 4. The validity of the public debt of the United States, authorized by law, including debts incurred for payment of pensions and bounties for services in suppressing insurrection or rebellion, shall not be questioned. But neither the United States nor any State shall assume or pay any debt or obligation incurred in aid of insurrection or rebellion against the united States, or any claim for the loss or emancipation of any slave; but all such debts, obligations and claims shall be held illegal and void.

Section 5. The Congress shall have power to enforce, by appropriate legislation, the provision of this article.

15th Amendment

[Proposed by Congress on February 26, 1869; ratification completed on February 3, 1870.]

Section 1. The right of citizens of the United States to vote shall not be denied or abridged by the United States or by any State on account of race, color, or previous condition of servitude.

Section 2. The Congress shall have power to enforce this article by appropriate legislation.

Name _____

Amendment Match

Review each statement below. Then next to the statement write the letter of the amendment or amendments to which the statement is referring.

    A. 13th Amendment   B.14th Amendment   C.15th Amendment

_____   1. Grants former male slaves the right to vote.

_____   2. Grants equal rights to all people born in the United States and those who became naturalized citizens.

_____   3. States that United States citizens cannot be stopped from voting based on race, color or previous condition of servitude.

_____   4. Outlaws former office holders of the Confederate government from serving in the United States Congress, or from holding other high offices in the United States government.

_____   5. Declares that involuntary servitude can exist as a punishment.

_____   6. States that the debts of the war incurred by the Union forces will be paid.

_____   7. Outlaws slavery.

_____   8. States that the cost of the war for the Confederate forces will not be paid by the United States government.

_____   9. Grants Congress the right to repeal the prohibition against Confederate soldiers or government officers from holding positions in the United States government or military.

_____   10. Grants Congress the power to enforce the amendment.

     Handout 8

Name _____

Amendment Review

1. What does the 13th Amendment outlaw? _____

   _____

   _____

2. Under what circumstances does the Constitution allow "involuntary servitude"?

   _____

   _____

3. What is the primary purpose for the 14th Amendment? _____

   _____

4. What two ways does the 14th Amendment allow people to become citizens?

   _____

5. According to the 14th Amendment, how does a person become a citizen of a state?

   _____

6. What are the three things states are prohibited from doing in Section 1 of the 14th Amend-

   ment? _____

   _____

7. According to the 14th Amendment, Section 2, what is an acceptable cause for which a state

   may abridge any voting rights? _____

   _____

8. According to Section 2 of the 14th Amendment, what is the punishment if a state denies
   voting rights to those citizens entitled to vote under the United States Constitution under

   the 14th Amendment? _____

   _____

   _____

   _____

   _____

Name _____

Amendment Review

TO PAY,
OR NOT TO PAY...
THAT IS
THE QUESTION!

9. What does Section 3 of the 14th Amendment limit? _____

10. What is the method for lifting the sanctions imposed against Confederate office holders?

   _____

11. What does Section 4 of the 14th Amendment state concerning the assumption of debts by

   the United States during the Civil War? _____

   _____

12. What does Section 4 of the 14th Amendment state concerning the debts of those by the

   people and governments in aid of the rebellion against the United States? _____

   _____

13. According to Section 4 of the 14th Amendment, will the United States pay for any claim for

   the loss or emancipation of any slave? _____

   _____

14. What is the subject of the 15th Amendment? _____

15. According to Section 1 of the 15th Amendment, what three characteristics cannot be used
    by the United States government or by the state governments to abridge or deny voting

    rights? _____

   _____

18   *Handout 9*

Name _____

The Poetry of Lincoln

Objectives

To understand poetry as primary source material.

Interpret symbolism used in poetry.

Vocabulary

metaphor: a figure of speech using an implied comparison, usually of two unlike things. Example: He's a bear in the mornings!

emancipate: set free

effigy: a likeness of a person, often used to burn or hang in protest.

martyr: a person killed because of his or her beliefs. Examples: Martin Luther King, Jr.; Joan of Arc.

Moses: biblical figure who led the Israelites out of slavery in Egypt to freedom and to the Promised Land, though, he died before the Israelites entered.

Background

The two poems in this section were written as commemoratives for events celebrating the Emancipation Proclamation and Lincoln himself. The first poem from A Poem, was written by James Monroe Whitfield for the fourth anniversary of the issuance of the Emancipation Proclamation. Whitfield (1822-1871) was an African American born in New Hampshire. Whitfield earned his living as a barber, though he was a prolific and impas-sioned writer for the abolition of slavery and for racial justice. This commemorative poem was 242 lines long, but only 20 lines of the original text are included here. These 20 lines are illustrative of his convincing and artful poetry.

The second poem, "The Emancipation Group," is a lesser known poem that John Greenleaf Whittier wrote in 1879 for the dedication of a statue of Abraham Lincoln erected in Boston. Whittier (1807-1892) was a Quaker whose abolitionist views were well known in his prose and poetry.

Both poems demonstrate the poets' reverence for Lincoln through metaphor and imagery.

Suggested Lesson Plan

1. Explain the lesson objectives.
2. Review the vocabulary and background information.
3. Read the excerpt of James Monroe Whitfield's poem aloud to the students.
4. Have students complete the activity sheet.
5. Read "The Emancipation Group" by John Greenleaf Whittier aloud to the students.
6. Have the students complete the activity sheet.

From <u>A Poem</u> by James Monroe Whitfield

Vocabulary

dross: worthless stuff or garbage.

"How Long"

by James Monroe Whitfield

[200]...
     Our real Moses, stretched his rod
          Four years ago across the sea,
     And through its blood-dyed waves we trod
          The path that leads to Liberty.
[205] His was the fiery column's light,
          That through the desert showed the way,
     Out of oppression's gloomy night,
          Toward the light of Freedom's day;
     And, like his prototype of old,
[210]   Who used his power, as heaven had told,
     To God and to the people true,
          Died with the promised land in view.
     And we may well deplore his loss,
          For never was a ruler given,
[215] More free from taint of sinful dross,
          To any Nation under Heaven,
     And ever while the earth remains,
          His name among the first shall stand
     Who freed four million slaves from chains,
[220]   And saved thereby his native land.
     ....

Name _____

Understanding A Poem
by James Monroe Whitfield

Use a dictionary to find the definition of the following word: ***dross***

1. To which biblical figure does Whitfield compare Lincoln?
   _____
   _____

2. How does the line, "Died with the promised land in view" relate to that comparison? _____
   _____

3. How is it true of Lincoln? _____
   _____

4. According to the poet, from where does Lincoln's power come? _____
   _____

5. What metaphor does the poet use to describe slavery?
   _____
   _____

6. What metaphor does the poet use to describe freedom?
   _____
   _____

7. According to the poem, what did Lincoln do by freeing the slaves? _____
   _____

8. Is Whitfield's poem favorable to Lincoln? Explain your answer. _____
   _____

"The Emancipation Group"

by John Greenleaf Whittier

[1]   Amidst thy sacred effigies
          Of old renown give place,
    O city, Freedom-loved! To his
          Whose hand unchained a race.

[2]   Take the worn frame, that rested not
          Save in a martyr's grave-
    The care-lined face, that none forgot,
          Bent to the kneeling slave.

[3]   Let man be free! The mighty word
          He spoke was not his own;
    An impulse from the highest stirred
          These chiseled lips alone.

[4]   The cloudy sign, the fiery guide,
          Along his pathway ran,
    And Nature, through his voice, denied
          The ownership of man.

[5]   We rest in peace where these sad eyes
          Saw peril, strife, and pain;
    His was the nation's sacrifice,
          And ours the priceless gain.

[6]   O symbol of God's will on earth
          As it is done above!
    Bear witness to the cost and worth
          Of justice and of love.

[7]   Stand in thy place and testify
          To coming ages long,
    That truth is stronger than a lie,
          And righteousness than wrong.

Name _____

Understanding "The Emancipation Group"

by John Greenleaf Whittier

Use a dictionary to find the definition of each of the following words:

emancipation _____

martyr _____

effigy _____

1. In the first stanza, how could a hand unchain a race?_____

    _____

2. What race was unchained? _____

3. To whom does the poet refer as a martyr? _____

    _____

4. In stanza 3, who does the poet say inspired the words, *let man be free?* _____

    _____

5. In stanza 4, through the flowery imagery, the poem again refers to slavery. What words are

    used to refer to it? _____

6. In stanza 5, Abraham Lincoln is described in two different ways. Use your own words to

    explain what the poem is saying. _____

    _____

7. In stanza 6, Lincoln is further compared. To what does the poem compare Lincoln? ____

    _____

8. Explain how the poem lets the reader know about whom the poem is written. _____

    _____

9. List two images of Lincoln used in the poem. _____

    _____

10. In your opinion, how would the poet view the line,

    "the pen is mightier than the sword"?_____

    _____

Editorial Cartoons

Objectives

Identify caricature.

Identify symbolism.

Draw conclusions about the meaning in a cartoon or print.

Identify differing opinions.

Draw own editorial cartoons.

Judge a cartoonist's viewpoint.

Vocabulary

rouge-et-noir: French meaning "red or black."

caricature: a drawing of a person that uses exaggerated features.

symbolism: when one thing (symbol) stands for or represents something else. Examples: the Liberty Bell in Philadelphia stands for freedom. The United States flag symbolizes the United States.

Background

Editorial cartoons make their editorial comments through art rather than writing. Even though most editorial cartoons contain writing, most of the message is to be found in the art. The cartoonist relies on the reader to understand the message in the cartoon. For this to happen, the reader has to be familiar with the story and the events relating to the cartoon. With prints and lithographs, like editorial cartoons, the imagery and symbolism is important for the viewer. To be able to understand the message, the viewer has to be able to unlock the message through the art in the print.

"Abe Lincoln's Last Card or Rouge-et-Noir" editorial cartoon published by *Punch* October 18, 1862 less than a month (September 22, 1862) after the Preliminary Emancipation Proclamation was issued. In the editorial cartoon, Lincoln with his moppish hair turned up into horns, is portrayed as a gambler with devilish intentions. The cartoon title, "Abe Lincoln's Last Card, or Rouge-et-Noir" indicated that Lincoln had run out of tricks to win the Civil War, so he issued the Preliminary Emancipation Proclamation to free the slaves in the states controlled by Confederate soldiers. In the cartoon, Lincoln plays his "devilish card game" with a Confederate soldier. The top of the card table rests on a gunpowder keg, indicating how explosive the gamble is. *Punch* was a magazine that appealed to the English nobility. This cartoon is also an indication that many of the English favored the southern defeat of the North and the dissolution of the United States. Some still harbored long resentments of the American defeat of the British during the American Revolution.

The prints, Volck and the Currier and Ives ("Freedom to the Slaves"), both address Lincoln and the Emancipation Proclamation but each has an entirely different message. Each uses symbolism to convey a point of view. The Currier and Ives print depicts Lincoln as a near biblical figure leading an entire race to freedom. The editorial cartoon, on the other hand, is full of overt symbolism and paints a near satanic Lincoln trampling on the Constitution as he dips his pen in devilish ink to write the Emancipation Proclamation.

"Writing the Emancipation Proclamation" was published around 1864, about a year after the Emancipation Proclamation was issued. This print was produced by a Copperhead printmaker, Adalbert Joann Volck. This is a very dark print portraying Lincoln as a man driven to signing the Proclamation because of devilish and alcoholic spirits. The imagery in the print leaves no doubt that the printmaker views the emancipation of slaves as a monumental and misguided mistake. Note the portrait of John Brown. In the portrait, John Brown is pictured with a halo, indicating sainthood. John Brown was an abolitionist who led a group that attacked a pro-slavery family named Doyle May 24, 1856, killing Pleasant Doyle and his two oldest sons. Later the same night, John Brown's group attacked and killed two more settlers. Three years later on October 16, 1859, Brown led 21 men to take the arsenal at Harpers Ferry. Federal forces, led by Robert E. Lee, retook the arsenal, killing most of Brown's men, and wounding Brown. Brown was hanged December 2 of that same year in Charles Town, Virginia. Also hanging on the wall behind Lincoln is a painting of

To the Teacher

TLC10349 Copyright © Teaching & Learning Company, Carthage, IL 62321-0010

Saint Domingue, portraying the slave revolt of 1791. The slaves attacked the plantation owners in an uprising where thousands of Haitians died—slaves and masters were brutally killed. This painting behind Lincoln portrays the victorious slaves dancing naked—gleeful in their debauchery. This image is used to frighten, insinuating that the freed slaves will rise up and murder the plantation owners of the South. The images of Satanism appear throughout the print—the vulture-headed curtain tie back, the inkstand held by a winged devil that Lincoln dipped his pen into to sign the Proclamation, the ram's head and cloven-hoofed desk legs. Other indicators of Volck's point of view against Lincoln and the Proclamation are Lincoln's foot on the United States Constitution (indicating that Volck believed that it was Lincoln trampling on states' constitutional rights to decide the slavery issue on their own), the decanter and liquor glasses indicating Lincoln might have been intoxicated when he signed the Proclamation and the baboon mask over the Liberty statue in the corner of the room.

In the print "Freedom to the Slaves" Lincoln is portrayed as a modern-day Moses. Like Moses, who led the Israelites to the Promised Land, Moses never entered. Lincoln, who led the Union to victory in the Civil War, never had the chance to savor the victory because John Wilkes Booth assassinated him just days after Lee surrendered. The caption underneath the print says, "Proclaimed January 1st, 1863, by Abraham Lincoln, President of the United States. "Proclaim liberty throughout All the land unto All the inhabitants thereof."—Lev. XXV. 10. The reference is to Leviticus, chapter 25, verse 10—"And ye shall hallow the fiftieth year, and proclaim liberty throughout all the lands unto all the inhabitants thereof: it shall be a jubile unto you; and ye shall return every man unto his possession, and ye shall return every man unto his family."

Clearly, Currier and Ives created a picture that was favorable to the fallen President Lincoln. The print is sentimental. It portrays Lincoln as a modern-day Moses who has led African Americans out of slavery to freedom. Lincoln is pointing to Heaven in this print, while an African American man kneels in front of Lincoln and kisses his hand. The man has been recently released from slavery—the shackles at his feet are opened. The woman looks on. The family is wearing tattered clothing but is clearly happy with their new station in life, happy to be together and grateful to Lincoln.

Suggested Lesson Plan

1. Explain the objectives of the lesson to the students.
2. Define the vocabulary, *caricature* and *rouge-et-noir*, for the students.
3. Distribute copies of the editorial cartoon that was published in *Punch*. Explain to the students that *Punch* was a British publication and the cartoonist was English. Also explain that the cartoon was published shortly after the Preliminary Emancipation was issued in September 22, 1862. The cartoon can be used by the students to be discussed with all of the students, or invite them to view the cartoon and fill in the answers.
4. Distribute copies of the two prints, "Freedom to the Slaves" and "Writing the Emancipation Proclamation."

    Have students describe the imagery in each print.

    Ask them how the imagery is different.

    Ask the students if there are any similarities.

    Is one print more positive toward Lincoln than the other?

    Which printmaker would the students think favored a southern victory?

    What clues in the print would lead them to that conclusion?
5. Distribute the review handouts and invite the students to answer the questions about each print.

Name _____

Understanding "Abe Lincoln's Last Card or Rouge-et-Noir"

Published in the English magazine Punch *on October 18, 1862.*

_____ 1. In the cartoon, Abraham Lincoln is portrayed as a
   a. saint　　　　　b. the devil　　　　　c. President of the United States

2. What clues in the cartoon leads you to the answer in question 1?_____

_____

_____ 3. In the card game, Lincoln is
   a. a Union soldier　　b. a British soldier　　c. a Confederate soldier

4. What clues in the cartoon leads you to the answer in question 1?_____

_____

_____ 5. The editorial cartoon was published shortly after Lincoln announced that he was going to emancipate the slaves. The cartoonist views the decision to free the slaves as
   a. a good idea by a wily　　　　　b. a desperate act to win the war
      politician whose time has come　　c. a brilliant but hopeless act

6. Explain how your answer relates to the title of the cartoon. _____

_____

7. In your opinion, what does the barrel of gunpowder represent? _____

_____

8. Do you agree with the cartoonist's point of view of the Emancipation Proclamation?

   Why or why not? _____

"Freedom to the Slaves"

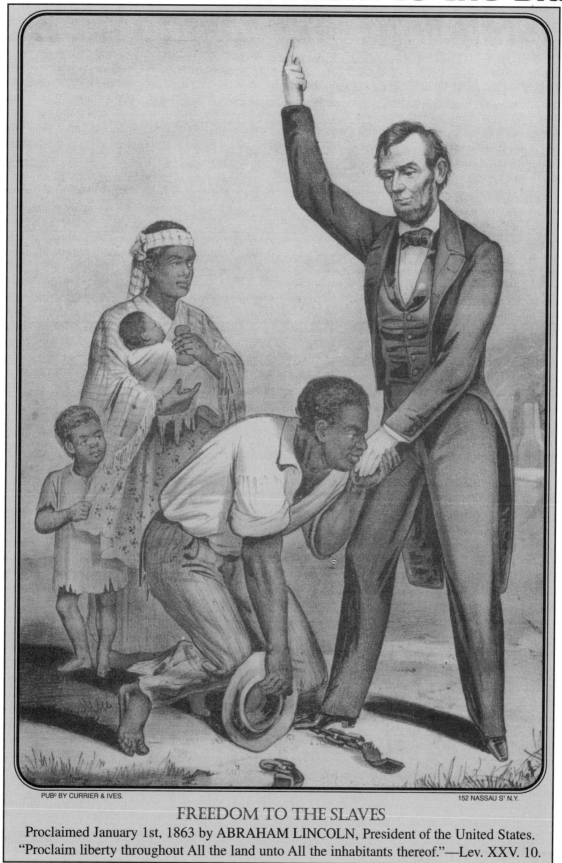

FREEDOM TO THE SLAVES

Proclaimed January 1st, 1863 by ABRAHAM LINCOLN, President of the United States.
"Proclaim liberty throughout All the land unto All the inhabitants thereof."—Lev. XXV. 10.

Courtesy of The Lincoln Museum, Fort Wayne, Indiana, (Ref. #2793)

By Currier & Ives, printed in about 1865.

Name _____

Understanding "Freedom to the Slaves"
by Currier & Ives

1. In the Bible verse, who is quoted as saying, "Proclaim liberty throughout All the land unto All the inhabitants thereof?" _____

2. What is the comparison being made between the biblical figure and Abraham Lincoln? __ _____

3. Why do you think Abraham Lincoln is pointing upwards? _____ _____

4. Note the broken shackles in the foreground of the print. What do they symbolize? _____

5. Who do the man, woman and children represent in the print? _____ _____

6. Why is the man bent on his knee kissing Lincoln's hand? _____ _____

7. Do you think the printmakers, Currier and Ives, portrayed Lincoln positively? Explain your answer. _____ _____

Beyond the Print

After the Civil War and for generations, African Americans belonged to the party of Lincoln. How does that statement relate to the print?

"Writing the Emancipation Proclamation"

By Adalbert Joann Volck, Baltimore, Maryland (c. 1864).

Courtesy of The Lincoln Museum, Fort Wayne, Indiana, (Ref. #3252)

Handout 17

Name _____

Understanding "Writing the Emancipation Proclamation"
by Adalbert Joann Volck

Note the many satanic symbols in this print—such as the ram's head at the corner of the table; the cloven hoof-footed table legs; the vulture-headed curtain tie back; and the most obvious—the devil whose arms are wrapped around the inkwell on the writing table. Other symbols in the print—a portrait of a sainted John Brown above Abraham Lincoln's head. To the right of Lincoln a painting of debauchery and evil. Behind Lincoln is a hooded figure representing Liberty. Bats fly outside the window. Alcohol is on the table.

1. What is the significance of Lincoln's foot resting on a book titled *U. S. Constitution?* _____

   _____

2. Research John Brown and his role at Harpers Ferry. How does the printmaker portray

   John Brown? _____

   _____

3. Does the printmaker portray John Brown's role at Harpers Ferry as positive or negative?

   _____

4. Is Lincoln's decision to issue the Emancipation Proclamation according to this printmaker,

   good or bad? Explain your answer. _____

   _____

5. What message does the imagery used in this print send to the viewer about Abraham Lin-

   coln? _____

   _____

6. In your opinion, is the printmaker for or against the issuance of the Emancipation Procla-

   mation? Explain your answer. _____

   _____

Beyond the Print
In this print, the printmaker has used satire to help make his point of view clear to the viewers. How does the printmaker use satire in his depiction with the portrait of John Brown?

_____

_____

Answer Key

The Emancipation Proclamation Time Line, page 9

November 1860	Abraham Lincoln elected President of the United States
December 1860	South Carolina secedes from the Union
February 1861	Confederate States adopt a Constitu-tion
April 1861	Fort Sumter attacked
September 1862	Preliminary Emancipation Proclamation issued
January 1863	Emancipation Proclamation issued

Civil War Map Activity, page 10

Read the Emancipation Proclamation Time Line handout and label the map.

Understanding the Emancipation Proclamation, page 12

1. Set free
2. An official announcement
3. September 22, 1862
4. January 1, 1863
5. Slaves in Confederate states were declared free; the United States government and the Union military forces will not prevent anyone who is trying to escape to freedom, but will lend them support.
6. Those states that took up arms against the United States government and formed their own confederate government.
7. States in which a majority of voters declare that they are not in rebellion.
8. Abraham Lincoln
9. President of the United States
10. To declare the freedom of those slaves who were living inside of Confederate States
11. The 11 states of the Confederate States, with exceptions for sections of Virginia and Louisiana.

12. The free states of the North and the slave states on the border—Delaware, Missouri, Kentucky and Maryland.
13. Lincoln was trying to keep them in the Union by not antagonizing any of the slaveholders in those states.
14. Since the United States government did not really have control over the Confederate States, the Emancipation Proclamation did not really free any slaves in those states. And in areas that were controlled by the federal government—such as Delaware, Maryland, Missouri and Kentucky—the proclamation did not free any of those slaves where the federal forces could have affected their freedom.
15. Abstain from violence and labor faithfully for fair wages.
16. They will be given positions in the armed forces.

Proclamation Crossword, page 13
1.   s l a v e s
2.   V i r g i n i a
3. e m a n c i p a t i o n
4. p r o c l a m a t i o n
5.   c o m m a n d e r i n c h i e f
6. r e b e l l i o n
7.   U n i o n

Amendment Match, page 16
1. C, 2. B, 3. C, 4. B, 5. A, 6. B, 7. A, 8. B, 9. B, 10. A, B and C

Amendment Review, pages 17-18
1. Slavery
2. As a punishment for a crime
3. Guarantee rights to former slaves
4. Birth or naturalized
5. To live or reside inside the boundaries of a state
6. Shall abridge the privileges or immunities of citizens of the United States; deprive any per-

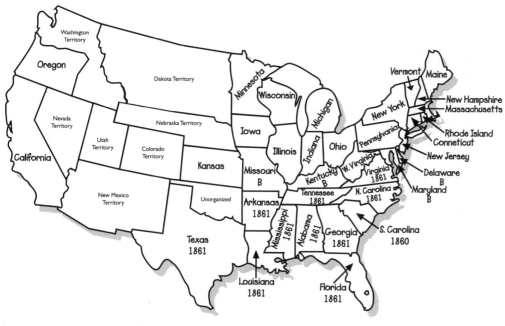

Answer Key

son of life, liberty or property without due process of law; deny to any person within its jurisdiction the equal protections of the law.

7. If one has participated in the civil war or some other crime
8. A state could lose representatives in the House of Representatives.
9. It limits the officers and military officers of the Confederate States from holding certain federal offices.
10. Two-thirds vote of Congress
11. Debts shall not be questioned.
12. Declares the debts invalid
13. No, such claims are to be held illegal and void.
14. Voting rights for former male slaves
15. Race, color or previous servitude

Understanding "A Poem," page 21

dross: worthless stuff or garbage

1. Moses
2. Moses led the Israelites from Egypt to the Promised Land, but Moses did not get to enter the Promised Land before he died. Lincoln led Union forces to defeat Confederate forces to win the Civil War but he did not get to live in the peace after the war.
3. Lincoln ended slavery for African Americans and had led the Union to victory over Confederate forces but never lived to enjoy the fruits of the victory.
4. From God
5. Oppression's gloomy night
6. The light of freedom's day
7. Saved his country, "saved thereby his native land."
8. Answers will vary but could include: Whitfield's poem is quite favorable to Lincoln. It compares him to one of the most important figures in the Bible. The poet also

indicates that Lincoln saved his nation and will forever be remembered by those whom he freed.

Understanding "The Emancipation Group," page 23

emancipation: set free

martyr: a person killed because of his or her beliefs

effigy: a likeness of a person, often used to burn or hang in protest

1. Lincoln unchained the race with his hand by signing the Emancipation Proclamation.
2. Those who had been enslaved, the African Americans
3. Abraham Lincoln
4. God
5. Ownership of man
6. The nation's sacrifice, priceless gain
7. God's will in justice and love
8. Answers will vary but could include: The association to Lincoln is clear because of the title; and the image of a martyr bent to the kneeling slave is clearly referring to Lincoln
9. Martyr, nation's sacrifice, symbol of God's will
10. Answers will vary but could include: since the poet speaks about a hand that unchained a race, the poet might be saying that Lincoln did more with the stoke of a pen by signing the Emancipation Proclamation than the soldiers had accomplished.

Understanding "Abe Lincoln's Last Card or Rouge-et-Noir," page 26

1. B
2. Lincoln's disheveled hair is turned up into horns
3. C
4. Lincoln's major opponents in the Civil War were Confederate soldiers
5. C
6. In the card game, often the last card played can determine the fate of the game.

7. Answers will vary but could include: the gunpowder of the explosives used in war; the explosive reaction from the Southerners to freeing the slaves; or the power released by freeing the slaves.
8. Answers will vary.

Understanding "Freedom to the Slaves," page 28

1. God
2. Moses led the Israelites out of Egypt; Lincoln led the slaves out of bondage to freedom.
3. He is pointing to Heaven.
4. The recent slavery of the African American
5. The slaves of the south
6. He is grateful to Lincoln for his family's freedom.
7. Answers will vary.

Beyond the Print, page 28

African Americans saw Lincoln and the Republican Party as liberators.

Understanding "Writing the Emancipation Proclamation," page 30

1. The artist is portraying Lincoln's Emancipation Proclamation as a trampling of the Constitution.
2. The artist portrays John Brown as a saint, note the halo.
3. The printmaker portrays John Brown as a saint, and at the same time portrays Lincoln as a supporter of John Brown's massacre.
4. Answers will vary, but could include: Bad, the clues are in the print. The printmaker portrays Lincoln as a satanic figure under the influence of evil spirits and trampling on the Constitution.
5. The printmaker believes Lincoln is evil.
6. Answers will vary but could include: The Printmaker is against the Emancipation Proclamation, illustrated by the images that he surrounds Lincoln with.

32